Contents

Chandelier Earrings, page 27

Simply Bead & Wire

LARK CRAFTS

An Imprint of Sterling Publishing
387 Park Avenue South
New York, NY 10016

If you have questions or comments about this book, please visit: larkcrafts.com

10 9 8 7 6 5 4 3

Published by Lark Crafts
An Imprint of Sterling Publishing Co., Inc.
387 Park Avenue South, New York, NY 10016

ISBN 978-1-4547-0024-1

First published in this format in 2011.
The material was previously published in the book *Contemporary Bead & Wire Jewelry* (ISBN 978-1-60059-590-5).

Distributed in Canada by Sterling Publishing, c/o Canadian Manda Group, 165 Dufferin Street, Toronto, Ontario, Canada M6K 3H6

Distributed in the United Kingdom by GMC Distribution Services,
Castle Place, 166 High Street, Lewes, East Sussex, England BN7 1XU

Distributed in Australia by Capricorn Link (Australia) Pty Ltd., P.O. Box 704, Windsor, NSW 2756 Australia

Square and round wire profiles

Bead & Wire
TECHNIQUES

Wire

Traditionally, wire made from sterling silver or gold has been a popular choice for bead and wire jewelry, but many other wire products may be used too. Metal craft wire is now available in a wide variety of colors; relative newcomers include anodized and dyed metals such as aluminum, or niobium, which you can use alone or combined in the same piece of jewelry. Still other kinds of wire include brass, nickel, copper, and even platinum. Unlike these more malleable metals, super-springy *memory wire,* made from base metal or sometimes stainless steel, can be stretched and permanently bent, but it will always retain its initial coiled silhouette.

Whatever the metal, most wire comes in a large range of sizes and shapes, or *profiles.* Gauge is a scale of measurement that indicates a wire's diameter: the higher the numeral, the finer the wire. (Memory wire is the exception; it's sold in sizes to fit the neck, wrist, or finger.) Page 63 lists some helpful information about wire gauges and their U.S. and U.K. specifications.

The projects in this book suggest that you use a specific size of wire, generally from 14 to 26 gauge. Using gauges other than those specified in the instructions is fine, but keep in mind that very thin wire, though easier to shape, isn't strong enough for a lot of heavy beads, and very thick wire isn't suitable for small-scale designs—not to mention the limitation of the size of a bead's hole. Wires of the same gauge will all feel a bit different to manipulate, because some metals are softer than others. However, wire stiffens a bit as you work with it, adding more support to your work. This process is called *work hardening;* if wire gets handled too much, it becomes brittle and breaks.

Silver and gold wires are made and sold in different hardnesses: *dead soft*, *soft*, and *half hard.* In most cases, our designers have recommended the appropriate silver or gold wire hardness for their projects; when in doubt, use half-hard wire. Avoid dead-soft wire; it's difficult to work with and won't retain shaping or angles.

Many of the projects use sterling silver wire, but wire made from an *alloy* (a blend of less expensive metals) is an acceptable substitute, especially for jewelry for everyday wear or for working an unfamiliar design or technique. It's a great idea to use practice wire (of a similar gauge and hardness) if you plan to make a piece of jewelry from very expensive wire. Any inexpensive alloy wire will do.

Depending on the metal, wire is sold many different ways: on spools, in prepackaged coils, by weight, and by length. Look for

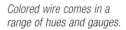
Colored wire comes in a range of hues and gauges.

Various gauges and types of wire
(from left): gold wire, memory wire,
and silver wire

various types in jewelry supply shops, craft retailers, and in certain areas of hardware stores (including the electrical supply and framing departments). The Internet is also a vast resource for wire of every kind.

In addition to the plain round variety, wire is made with different cross-section profiles, such as square, half round, and triangular. Some wire companies sell lengths of pretwisted single-strand wire, or you can make your own with the pin vise tool, as explained later on. Twisted wire is also created when two lengths of nonround wire are twisted together for a beaded or rippled effect. Although most of the projects in this book are made with the common round variety, a few, such as the Beaded Channel Ring on page 31, use these novelty shapes, which create a completely different look. It's possible to alternate links of round, flat, and twisted wire with stunning results.

Festive Spiral Earrings, page 58

Lantern Earrings,
page 56

Wire Techniques

Now for the fun: learning how to wrangle the wire into a great jewelry design using basic wire techniques. Unless you're already familiar with them, you'll probably want to practice these techniques with a low-cost wire first—it's not easy to straighten wire once it's bent the wrong way. You might want to use the fun colored-wire products to make your learning curve more enjoyable. The results might be good enough to use for a later project.

Sometimes it may seem as if your wire has a mind of its own. To keep spooled wire under control, put it in a small plastic storage bag. Pull out a length of wire as needed. If you're working with a coil of wire rather than a spool, wrap a piece of masking tape around it so it can't spring open in all directions. Good-looking jewelry pieces are those with smooth and confident swoops, angles, and curves, made from kink-free wire.

Straightening

To keep it in good condition, wire is stored and sold in coils. Coiling wire saves space, but it's best to straighten out its curve before you begin working with it. To straighten a short length of wire, hold one end of it with chain-nose pliers. Just above the pliers, grasp the wire with a cloth or paper towel to keep your hands clean and to prevent friction burn. Squeezing your fingers slightly, pull the length of wire through them.

If the wire bends or crimps at any time, gently run your finger along it to smooth the kink, or rub the wire over the edge of a table padded with newspaper. Don't smooth a crimp too vigorously, or the wire could break. (Shaping wire, remember, hardens it. The more it's worked, the more brittle it becomes.)

Wrapping

No matter what you're wrapping the wire around, always pull it tightly against the pliers, mandrel, bead, or wire. When you're making jump rings, keep each pass of the wire as even and as close to the last one as possible.

Using Jump Rings

Always open and close jump rings by holding each end with pliers and twisting one ring's end toward you and the other end away, as shown in figure 1; pulling the ends straight apart, laterally, will distort the ring's shape and can undermine the strength of the wire and cause it to break.

FIGURE **1**

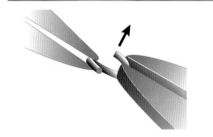

HANDMADE JUMP RINGS

To make your own jump rings, simply wind a length of wire tightly around a mandrel. If you want to make a lot of jump rings at once, you might consider using an eggbeater drill to quickly do the job. Secure both the mandrel and one end of the wire tightly in the tool's jaws. As you turn the handle, hold the wire close to the mandrel. Whether you use a drill or not, keep the rounds of wire as straight and as close to each other as possible. After you've wound all the wire, slide the coil you've just formed off the mandrel and trim the ends. Use wire cutters, in exactly the same position each time, to free a fully circular ring—no more, no less—from the coil. One last tip: it's tempting to use your fingers to pry open a jump ring, but avoid splitting your nails by using two pairs of flat-nose pliers instead.

Spirals

To create flat spirals, use the tip of a pair of round-nose pliers to curve one end of the wire into a half-circle or hook shape about ⅛ inch (0.3 cm) in diameter (see figure 2). Use the very tips of the pliers to curve the end of the wire tightly into itself, as shown in figure 3, aiming to keep the shape round rather than oval. Hold the spiral in flat- or chain-nose pliers and push the loose end of the wire against the already-coiled form (see figure 4); as you continue, reposition the wire in the pliers as needed.

FIGURE 3

FIGURE 2

FIGURE 4

Jelllyroll Bracelet, page 60

5

Lucky Necklace, page 25

Links and Loops

A *link* is simply one unit in a piece of jewelry. A link can be formed either by hand or with a jig. It can be an elaborate wire shape full of curls and curlicues or be based on a simple form, such as an S shape or a figure eight.

A *loop* is an important part of a link. The perfect loop should be precisely circular, centered over the straight part of the wire from which it's formed, and it should close tightly. Perfect your technique by making loops from different gauges of scrap wire.

Start with 6 inches (15.2 cm) of wire and work with a pair of round-nose pliers. Make a sharp 90-degree bend about ½ inch (1.3 cm) from one end of the wire, as shown in figure 5. This measurement will vary, depending on how large a loop you want to make; with practice, you'll get to know how much wire to allow for it.

Hold the wire so that the longer portion points to the floor and the short, bent end is pointing at you. Grasp the short end with the round-nose pliers, holding the pliers so that the back of your hand faces you. The closer to the tips you work, the smaller the loops you can make. Keeping the tips themselves stationary, rotate the pliers up and away from you (see figure 6). Be careful not to pull out the right-angle bend you made earlier. Stop rotating when you've made half the loop.

Slide the pliers' tips back along the wire a bit and resume the rotation. To prevent the loop from becoming misshapen, make sure to keep one of the pliers' tips snugly inside the loop as you make it, so that the loop is being formed by a combination of rotation and shaping around the "mandrel" of the pliers. Keep working, sliding the pliers back as needed, until the loop is closed against the 90-degree bend (see figure 7). To make all your loops look nice and consistent, see the Same-Sized Loops (Every Time!) sidebar on page 7.

A *bead loop link* is made by enclosing a bead between two loops. Another option is to start with an eye pin, so that you'll have to fashion only one closing loop.

FIGURE **5**

FIGURE **6**

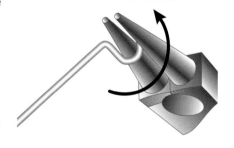

FIGURE **7**

Sante Fe Cuff, page 45

Sante Fe Cuff, page 45

FIGURE 8

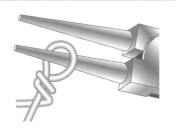

FIGURE 9

SAME-SIZED LOOPS (EVERY TIME!)

With a permanent marker, draw a line on the jaw of your round-nose pliers. If you place the wire there every time you make a loop, you can count on it always to be the same size.

Of course, there are hundreds of variations of these basic links. Links can be attached to each other with jump rings or linked directly together as you make them.

A *wrapped bead loop* is a simple variation of the bead loop link just described. Use an extra length of wire for the 90-degree bend. Once you've made the loop, reposition the pliers so that the lower jaw is inside it. Use your other hand to wrap the wire's tail around the base of the loop several times, as shown in figure 8. Slide on one or more beads and, if the design calls for it, repeat the loop-forming process at the other end to make a *wrapped bead loop link* (see figure 9). Trim off any excess wire.

Opening and Closing Loops

Just as with jump rings, use two pair of pliers to open and close loops. Twist the cut end sideways while keeping the other side of the loop stationary. Pulling it open

any other way will distort the loop's shape. Be sure to tighten any gaps in loops after you've attached your links.

Twisting

Only square wire can be twisted. Round wire won't show the twisting properly, and the process will just work-harden it.

To create twisted wire in no time at all, work with a pair of pin vises. Insert each end of a piece of wire into a pin vise, tighten the chucks, and twist them in opposite directions until you like the look you've achieved. If you have only one pin vise, secure the other end of the wire in a clamp or table vise (or in a pair of pliers if you have just a short quantity to twist). You can also use this tool to twist two lengths of the same wire together, creating a heavier look, or to twist together two different colors of wire.

Beaded Channel Ring,
page 31

Jig-Formed Links

A jig tool helps you make the same wire shape (usually a link) consistently, over and over. To keep your links identical, always follow the same circuit on the jig and try to work in the same manner each time. Using flat-nose pliers, hold a piece of wire tightly at one end, or place its tail in an empty hole in the jig that's near the first peg (or nail). Wrap the wire tightly around the pegs, following the pattern indicated in the instructions. Once you've made one unit, remove it from the jig and repeat to make all the units that you need. It's that easy.

Polishing

You can polish your jewelry with a jewelry buffing cloth (sometimes called a *rouge cloth*) or papers, which are available from most jewelry suppliers. Before using any cleaning solution, test it on a scrap piece of wire first. A tumbler is an option for some pieces, but make sure you're familiar with its operation and consider that many beads aren't suitable for the process.

The Needle Arts

Crocheting and knitting with wire aren't all that different from the yarn variety—and you needn't worry about your project shrinking in the wash later. Because wire is thinner and more slippery than yarn, the techniques may feel a little awkward at first. Even if you already have experience, you'll find that when using wire, you'll need to use a light hand in establishing the tension (i.e., how tightly or loosely the material is woven together), because this material has no elasticity whatsoever.

Creating a slipknot requires a different approach than with yarn, since wire doesn't actually slip. Instead of pulling on one end to tighten it, tug on both. The wire loop should still be able to move easily up and down the needle or hook. As you work, resist the temptation to wrap the wire around your finger, as is typical when working with yarn, because it will create even more kinks and crimps. And although you can smooth the kinks somewhat, don't worry too much about them, because for the most part they won't be noticeable in the finished piece.

Often, all the beads in a project are threaded onto the wire before you cast

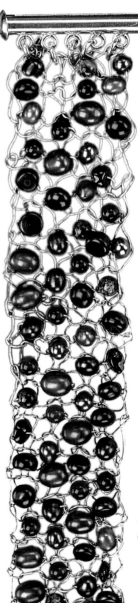

Mardi Gras Bracelet,
page 36

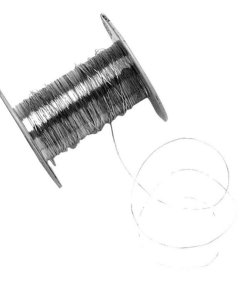

on, and then each one slipped into place as needed (usually after each stitch). As you cast on, be prepared to leave a tail long enough to finish the piece and hold the clasp.

Colored craft wire is popular for knitting and crocheting. If you'd like to try working with silver wire, consider using gold or *fine* silver wire, which is softer and lighter (though more expensive) than sterling.

Knitting

The projects in this book use only the knit or purl stitches, and they employ the standard knitting abbreviations you're used to seeing for yarn projects. Pull your knitting down and away from the needle as you go, flattening it slightly with your fingers, so as to make it easier to work the next row. Knitting needles come in different diameters and materials. Aluminum needles are more practical than wood or bamboo, simply because the wire will slip better on them, but what's most important is to use the size listed in the instructions in order to reproduce the project closely. Short, double-pointed needles are sometimes recommended for smaller-size pieces.

Crocheting

Crochet hooks also come in different sizes and may be aluminum, wood, or plastic; you can use a hook made from any material you like. Hook size affects how tightly or loosely woven the fabric appears between stitches, so if you want to duplicate the project, make sure to use the size specified in the instructions.

The only two crochet stitches used to create the projects in this book are the simplest ones—chain stitch and single crochet. Crocheted chain has a tendency to twist, so be prepared to do some smoothing as you work. Hold the loop you're working on with the thumb and finger of your nondominant hand so you can control its size and shape.

Time for lots of beady, loopy fun! You have a basic tool kit, some wire, and an exciting array of handpicked beads; you've practiced the techniques and know a wrapped loop from a bead link. You're ready for the rewarding handicraft of making bead and wire jewelry, and we have 23 delightful projects waiting.

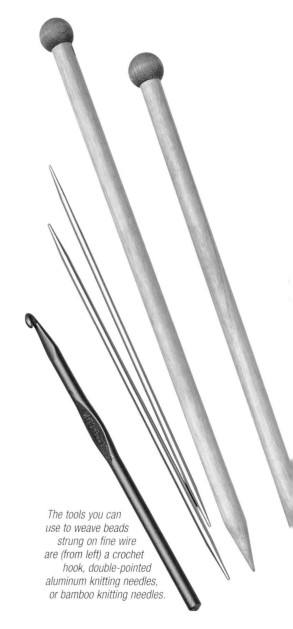

The tools you can use to weave beads strung on fine wire are (from left) a crochet hook, double-pointed aluminum knitting needles, or bamboo knitting needles.

Long, dangling earrings
are in vogue. Fine-gauge
silver wire and tiny,
twinkling glass beads
give these earrings a
cool, airy style.

Rachel Dow, Designer

Confetti Hoop Earrings

MATERIALS

48 gemstone beads in various colors, 3 to 4 mm diameter

26-gauge dead-soft sterling silver wire, 4 feet (1.2 m) long

8 jump rings, 16-gauge sterling silver, 10 mm diameter

6 jump rings, 18-gauge sterling silver, 6 mm diameter

2 sterling silver ear wires

INSTRUCTIONS

MAKE 2.

1 Using flush cutters, cut four pieces of 26-gauge wire, each 5¼ inches (13.3 cm) long.

2 Wrap one piece of 26-gauge wire twice around a 10-mm jump ring to secure it; using chain-nose pliers to grasp the thinner wire will help you get a tight wrap. Add a bead to the wire, hold it in place on the outer edge of the 10-mm jump ring, and wrap the wire tightly around the jump ring twice, being careful not to kink the light wire as you work.

3 Add another bead to the wire and continue wrapping and adding beads, working your way around the jump ring until you've attached six evenly spaced beads to it. Secure the tail of the wire by wrapping it tightly twice around the jump ring, close to the point where you began the wrapping. Cut off any extra wire.

4 Repeat steps 2 and 3 to make a total of four bead-wrapped 10-mm jump rings.

5 Use a fingernail or the tip of chain-nose pliers to separate the beginning/end wraps of wire on one of the bead-wrapped jump rings, and attach an ear wire there.

6 Using three 6-mm jump rings, link three more bead-wrapped jump rings sequentially to the one with the ear wire.

These delicate, lightweight earrings can dress up or dress down. Whatever the occasion, their design will be to your jewelry box what your black dress is to your wardrobe.

Ellen Gerritse, Designer

Whisper Drops Earrings

MATERIALS

18 sterling silver seed beads

18 white-frost twisted tube beads, 12 mm long

18 sterling silver crimp beads

18 sterling silver eye pins, 1 inch (2.5 cm) long

2 sterling silver ear wires

INSTRUCTIONS

MAKE 2.

1 Slip one eye pin onto another eye pin, then a seed bead, a tube bead, and a crimp bead. Close the crimp bead onto the beaded eye pin, ½ inch (1.3 cm) from the end.

2 Add another eye pin to the element you made in step 1, with the same sequence of beads and ending in a crimp bead.

3 Repeat steps 1 and 2 to make two more beaded elements.

4 Hang all three elements on an ear wire loop.

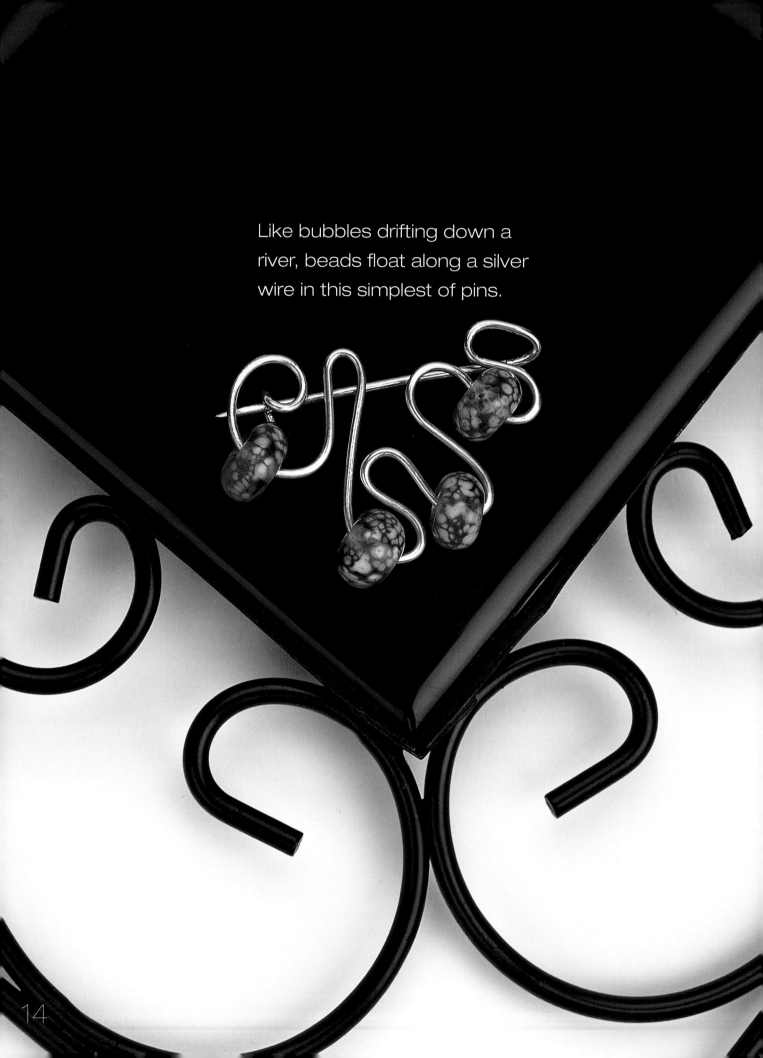

Like bubbles drifting down a river, beads float along a silver wire in this simplest of pins.

Silver Flow Brooch

Rachel Dow, Designer

MATERIALS

4 round glass beads, 5 mm diameter

16-gauge dead-soft sterling silver wire,
10 inches (25.4 cm) long

INSTRUCTIONS

1 Straighten the wire. Make a loop on one end to use later for making a hook for the pin stem.

2 Shape the wire to match figure 1, adding the beads as you work. After you shape the brooch, 1¾ inches (4.4 cm) of unbent wire should remain. File the end of this wire to a gradual taper for the pin stem, making the pin's point ¼ inch (0.6 cm) long.

3 To make the hook for the brooch, open the loop from step 1 with chain-nose pliers. Bend it at a right angle to the brooch.

4 Use round-nose pliers to bend the pin stem toward the hook. The pin stem should extend beyond the hook by ¼ inch (0.6 cm); make adjustments as necessary.

FIGURE **1**

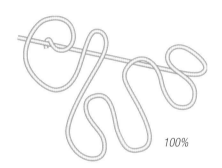

100%

Elegant twisted gold
wire frames a large
pendant of gleaming
amber, with a delicate
freshwater pearl
accenting the whole.
The designer was
lucky enough to find
a chunk of amber with
a tiny insect preserved
inside it.

Michaelanne Hall, Designer

Caught-in-Honey Pendant

MATERIALS

1 small freshwater pearl, 3 to 4 mm diameter

1 piece of amber, 20 to 25 mm diameter

1 gold bead, 2 mm diameter

24-gauge half-hard 14-karat gold round wire, 1½ inches (3.8 cm) long, for hanging the pearl

22-gauge soft 14-karat gold-filled square wire, 32 inches (81.3 cm) long, for the decorative wirework

20-gauge half-hard 14-karat gold half-round wire, 4½ inches (11.4 cm) long, for the wraps

TOOLS

Masking tape

Round dowel, 6 mm diameter

INSTRUCTIONS

1 Working with the 24-gauge wire and needle-nose pliers, turn ⅟₁₆ inch (0.2 cm) at one end and pinch it against the rest of the wire to make a tiny eye. String the gold bead and the pearl on the wire. Make a wrapped bead loop above the pearl.

2 Cut four pieces of 22-gauge wire, each 8 inches (20.3 cm) long. Mark the center of only one of the wires and use round-nose pliers to bend it into a U. Measure and mark ³⁄₁₆ inch (0.5 cm) from the bottom of the U and bend the wire 90 degrees there, to look like figure 1. Slide the pearl element made in step 1 onto the U.

3 Place the four 22-gauge wires together, side by side, with the U-shaped wire in an inner position. Cut two pieces of 20-gauge wire, each 1 inch

(2.5 cm) long. On either side of the U, wrap these three times around all the 22-gauge wires, making sure to keep them side by side as you wrap. Trim any excess 20-gauge wire, so that the ends are on the side opposite the U bend.

4 Holding the wrapped area gently with needle-nose pliers, twist both ends of the inner wire that's *not* the U wire.

5 Place one end of the amber against the wrapped quartet of wires and use your fingers to curve them against

FIGURE 1

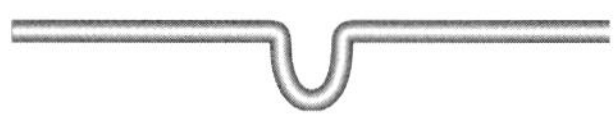

Caught-in-Honey Pendant

FIGURE **2**

Back

4 3

2

1

the stone. Referring to figure 2, hold your work so that the U-shaped wire is in the #2 position. Shape both ends of the twisted wire (#3) along either side of the amber piece. Snug wire #1 over the front of the amber piece, and wire #4 around the back. Shape wire #2 so that it gently curves no more than ⅛ inch (0.3 cm) away from the amber.

6 Collect all the wires at the top of the pendant, making certain that they hold the amber securely. Wrap masking tape around them, about 1 inch (2.5 cm) above where you will bind them. Cut a piece of 20-gauge wire 2½ inches (6.4 cm) long and, working from bottom to top, bind the wires together securely by wrapping the wire four times around them. Trim any excess wire on the back side of the pendant.

7 Remove the masking tape. Evenly divide the wires into two groups of four, making certain the group on the right side of the pendant contains two wires that aren't twisted. Arrange the wires in this set side by side, making sure the two outer wires are not twisted ones.

8 Still working from the right side of the pendant, twist the two inner wires. Use your fingers to shape the four wire ends across the front of the amber, then around the outside of wire #2. Hook their ends around wire #2 and clip off any excess wire.

9 Select two of the remaining four wire ends at the top of the pendant and bend them straight down over the back of the binding. Clip the wires ⅜ inch (1 cm) long. Turn under the ends and tuck them between the binding and the stone.

10 Use the remaining wires to make the bail. Twist the ones that aren't already twisted. Place the dowel behind them, right above the binding. Hold the wires against the dowel with your thumb and bend the wires slightly toward you. Wrap the left-hand wire away from you and to the left twice around the dowel. Repeat with the wire on the right so that it mirrors the left side. Remove the dowel and pinch the wraps close together.

11 Bring the left-hand wire of the bail down to wrap around wire #2, near the shoulder of the pendant. Clip any extra wire. Working from front to back, wrap the bail's right-hand wire twice around the top of the four wires that cross the front of the amber. Snip off any excess wire.

Fiesta Necklace and Earrings

Kate Drew-Wilkinson, Designer

The energetic color combination of this set gives the impression you're wearing a party!

Fiesta Necklace and Earrings

MATERIALS FOR THE NECKLACE

22 red ceramic donut beads, ½ inch (1.3 cm) diameter

27 turquoise round ceramic beads, 8 mm diameter

57 antique copper heishi spacer beads

54 sterling silver round beads, 2.5 mm diameter

20-gauge half-hard silver wire, 6 feet (1.8 m) long

4 silver ball-end head pins, 2 inches (5.1 cm) long

1 pierced silver pendant, 3.5 x 4.5 cm

1 silver S-clasp

FINISHED LENGTH

25½ inches (64.8 cm)

INSTRUCTIONS

1 Set aside 7 donut beads, 11 round ceramic beads, 19 spacers, and 20 sterling silver beads.

2 Cut the wire into 3-inch (7.6 cm) pieces. Using one piece of wire, make a wrapped bead loop link with a sterling silver bead, a spacer, a round ceramic bead, another spacer, and another sterling silver bead on it. Slip a donut on a loop before closing it. Keep the loops large enough to allow the donut free movement.

3 Make another wrapped bead loop link threaded with the same beads as in step 2, slipping the donut from the previous link onto one loop and adding another donut to the loop at the other end. Repeat the process until you've used all the beads except those set aside in step 1. Slip the ends of the S-clasp onto the free loops at the beginning and end of the strand, closing the necklace.

4 Using the beads set aside in step 1, make a bead loop link threaded with the same beads as in step 2. Before closing the second loop, attach it to the sixth donut from the clasp. Repeat, attaching a bead loop link to the next four donuts. Make and attach two more bead loop links on the eighth donut.

5 Make a bead loop link threaded with a sterling silver bead, a spacer, and another sterling silver bead, adding the silver pendant to one loop; attach the other loop to the center link hanging on the eighth donut.

6 Thread a turquoise bead, a spacer, and a sterling silver bead on each ball-end head pin. Attach one each to the fifth and eleventh donuts, and the last two at the ends of the two links on the eighth donut.

MATERIALS FOR THE EARRINGS

20 sterling silver round beads, 2.5 mm diameter

20 copper heishi spacer beads

8 red ceramic donut beads, ½ inch (1.3 cm) diameter

6 turquoise ceramic beads, 8 mm diameter

20-gauge half-hard silver wire, 2 feet (61 cm)

2 ear wires

INSTRUCTIONS

MAKE 2.

1 Cut the wire into 3-inch (7.6 cm) pieces.

2 Make two wrapped bead loop links, threading a sterling silver bead, three spacers, and another sterling silver bead on each; slip an ear wire on one loop end and a donut on the other. Keep one of the loops large enough to allow the donut free movement.

3 Make another wrapped bead loop link with a sterling silver bead, a spacer, and another sterling silver bead threaded on it, attaching one loop to the donut from the previous step and leaving the other loop empty.

4 Make a bead loop link like the ones from step 2 for the necklace. Before closing the loops, attach a donut to one of them, then link the other loop to the empty end of the link from the previous step. Repeat two more times.

The deep, iridescent jewel tones in this brooch charmingly capture one of nature's prettiest flying creatures. Colored wire skillfully ties together the overall color scheme.

Beaded Dragonfly Brooch

Mami Laher, Designer

MATERIALS

250 assorted seed beads in blues, greens, iridescent, and crystal

2 faceted iridescent beads, 4 mm diameter

2 round crystal beads, 8 mm diameter

18-gauge green wire, 20 inches (50.8 cm) long

22-gauge blue or purple wire, 20 inches (50.8 cm) long

28-gauge wire in color of your choice, 56 inches (1.4 m) long

Small pin back

Jewelry glue (optional)

INSTRUCTIONS

Note: Use pliers with plastic-coated jaws, or wrap metal jaws with duct tape, to protect the colored wire from scratches.

1 Shape the green wire into the dragonfly shape with round-nose pliers, using figure 1 as a template. Start at the head, making the first bend 1½ inches (3.8 cm) from one end to form the small V between the eyes. Shape symmetrical eye loops on either side of the bend, using round-nose pliers.

2 Make the U bend for the tail in the long end of the wire, 2½ inches (6.4 cm) below the eyes.

3 Holding the dragonfly body near its center, make the loop for the top right wing first, ½ inch (1.3 cm) below the eyes. Shape the other wings in a figure-eight motif. Make the bottom wings slightly longer than the top wings if you wish. The wingspan should be 2½ inches (6.4 cm) when you are finished.

FIGURE 1

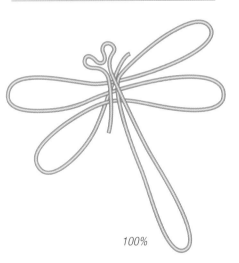

100%

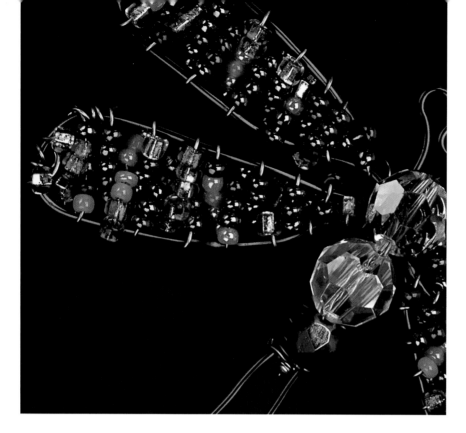

Beaded Dragonfly Brooch

4 Push the wire's ends back toward the center of the body so they clasp the loose frame a bit tighter, but don't twist them. (You will wrap the body to hold it tighter in the next step.) Shorten the ends if necessary. Smooth, torque, and flatten the framework with flat-nose piers.

5 Using the blue or purple wire, hold the pin back against the framework, a short distance from the head, and wrap the thorax area from top to bottom. (Keep the pin back open so that the wire binds only the spine of the pin back.) Make a couple of X-shaped wraps where the wings intersect, to stabilize them, as you go. Keep the wrapping as neat and flat as possible. Check often to be sure that the pin back can still close.

6 Cut 12 inches (30.5 cm) of 28-gauge wire. Anchor one end near the base of the first wing by tucking it into the wire wrapping on the body.

Wrap it once around the base of the wing, then add the first seed bead. (Spill the seed beads onto a woven dishtowel or other fabric to control them.)

7 Work back and forth across the wing, toward the tip, using a snug figure-eight wrap (i.e., over and under the frame in an alternating pattern). Add just enough seed beads to the beading wire to fill the space each time you wrap, snugging each line of beading against the one before it. Add beads in rows of related colors, occasionally punctuating the wing with one or two especially brilliant or sparkly beads. The outermost tip of the wing has two beads sitting atop the frame, with extra wire wraps. If you can, run the tail end of the beading wire back through one of the beads, then clip any excess. Use your pliers to put a tiny curve in the wire end and press it between the beads.

8 Repeat steps 6 and 7 for the remaining three wings.

9 Use the rest of the 28-gauge wire for the final embellishing. Fold the wire into a narrow U shape and position it under the body, just below the pin back; bring its ends to the front and twist them firmly together. Thread a 4-mm iridescent bead onto the pair of wires and push it down on the twisted wire, against the body. Twist the wires together several times until you have one strong wire that stretches to the neck. Add the two crystal beads onto the twisted wire. They should cover the area where the wings adjoin the body; if not, add another 4-mm iridescent bead before adding the crystal ones.

10 Wrap the two separate ends of the wire behind the neck of the dragonfly. Cinch everything together by twisting the ends behind the neck. Cut the excess wire, leaving ½ inch (1.3 cm) of twisted wire curved and tucked behind larger wires. If you wish, you can control the position of the embellishment beads and the wire ends with a small drop or two of jewelry glue.

Lucky Necklace

Mami Laher, Designer

The carved charm on this spectacular necklace might attract good fortune. Though the bead links look ornate, they consist of just a few simple elements.

Lucky Necklace

MATERIALS

25 assorted honey-colored glass beads, 5 mm

4 dichroic glass cube beads, 9 mm

12 faceted beads, 1 cm

4 rondelles, 1 cm

2 flat stone beads, 1 inch (2.5 cm) diameter

1 round carved charm, 1¾ inches (4.4 cm) diameter

20-gauge gold-filled square wire, 49 inches (1.2 m) long, for the caged bead links

22-gauge gold-filled square wire, 48 inches (1.2 m) long, for the caged bead links

18-gauge gold-filled wire, 27 inches (68.6 cm) long, for making bead loop links

16-gauge gold-filled wire, 4¼ inches (10.8 cm) long, for the clasp and a connection element

28 jump rings, 18-gauge gold filled, 5 mm diameter

2 jump rings, 18-gauge gold filled, 9 mm diameter

1 jump ring, 18-gauge gold filled, 3 mm diameter

TOOLS

Tabletop vise

Hammer and block

FINISHED LENGTH

27 inches (68.6 cm)

INSTRUCTIONS

1. Cut and twist four pieces of 20-gauge square wire, each 8 inches (20.3 cm) long.

2. Cut two pieces of twisted wire, each 3½ inches (8.9 cm) long. Cut one piece of untwisted 20-gauge square wire 4¼ inches (10.8 cm) long. Slip two 5-mm beads on each twisted wire and one glass cube on the untwisted wire and place them side by side, as shown in figure 1, shaping the wires into bundles at the ends.

3. Cut two pieces of 22-gauge square wire, each 6 inches (15.2 cm) long. Clamp the end of one in the vise and wrap the other end four times around one of the bundled wire ends; repeat for the other end. Make spirals out of all six wire ends. Repeat the process to make a total of four caged-bead links.

4. Using the 18-gauge wire, make bead loop links out of each faceted bead, rondelle, stone bead, and the remaining 5-mm beads.

5. To make the clasp, use a piece of 16-gauge wire 2¼ inches (5.7 cm) long. Shape it as shown in figure 2, then forge the large outside curves. Adjust the clasp's form if the hammer's blows distort it.

6. To assemble one side of the chain, attach the links with 5-mm jump rings. For the caged bead links, pass the jump ring through the spiral of the center wire. The parts are assembled with faceted beads alternating a caged bead, a stone, a caged bead, and ending with two rondelles and two 5-mm beads. On the end with a 5-mm bead, attach the clasp with a jump ring.

7. Make a second chain, as described in the previous step, but on the end with the 5-mm bead, use a 5-mm jump ring to attach a 9-mm jump ring.

8. An extra length of chain will be added to the 9-mm jump ring. To make it, link together the five remaining bead loops by their loops. Use the 3-mm jump ring to hang one end of the chain to the 5-mm jump ring.

9. Cut a piece of 16-gauge wire 2 inches (5.1 cm) long and shape it to look like figure 3. Use the remaining 9-mm jump ring to hang the charm from the central loop of this element. Attach a chain through the center of each spiral with a 5-mm jump ring.

FIGURE 1

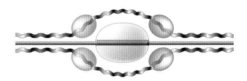

FIGURE 2

FIGURE 3

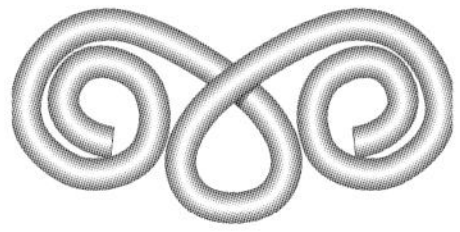

Chandelier Earrings

Eni Oken, Designer

Beaded tendrils dangle from a larger bead that's framed by an unusual herringbone weave. The result is an airy design—daringly long yet light as a feather.

Chandelier Earrings

INSTRUCTIONS

1 Make the central dangles. Cut two pieces of 26-gauge wire 3 inches (7.6 cm) long each. Slip a ½-inch (1.3 cm) flat pear on each of them and use a 1-inch (2.5 cm) tail to make wrapped bead loops, trimming the tails' excess.

2 With the remaining wire and round-nose pliers, form small wrapped loops as close as possible to the ones you just made. Wind the wire on top of the previous wrapping; this gives the fine wire a more substantial appearance. Trim the wires closely.

3 Cut two pieces of 26-gauge wire 3 inches (7.6 cm) long. Make two wrapped loop bead links with a 9-mm rondelle on each, catching a ½-inch (1.3 cm) flat pear dangle at one end of each of the links. Trim off any extra wire.

4 Make the four side dangles, as you did in steps 1 and 2, using ½-inch (1.3 cm) flat pears instead.

5 Fabricate four smaller dangles from 4-inch (10.2 cm) lengths of 26-gauge wire. Make four wrapped bead loop links with two 5-mm beads each, catching a dangle from step 4 in one end of each. Trim away any extra wire.

6 Cut a piece of 24-gauge wire 4 inches (10.2 cm) long. Make a wrapped loop near one end of it, wrapping as many times as it takes to create a shank ¼ inch (0.6 cm) long. (Counting the number of times you wrap will help you replicate the shank on the opposite side of the bead.)

7 Slip a 10-mm rondelle onto the working end of the wire and make another ¼-inch (0.6 cm) shank with a wrapped loop on the other end of the wire, attaching the dangle you made in step 1 into the loop before you wrap it

closed (see figure 1). Trim the ends of the wires with a flush cutter.

8 To craft a herringbone weave around the 10-mm rondelle, cut a piece of 26-gauge wire 2½ feet (76.2 cm) long. Secure the wire by wrapping it twice around one of the shanks, near the bead. Trim the tail. Bring the working wire down one side of the bead, and clockwise around the shank, from front to back, positioning the wire as close to the bead as possible; do the same on the other side of the bead. This completes one entire herringbone weave around the bead.

9 Repeat to complete five full weaves around the bead. As you progress, snug the wire against the bead's sides.

10 Weave the top of a sixth herring-bone, but before wrapping the wire on the lower shank, slip one of the smaller-bead dangles onto the wire. Twist a small loop at the 4 o'clock position. After weaving the wire around the lower shank, make another small loop at the 8 o'clock position for another dangle. Bring the wire to the top shank, wrap it tightly twice around it, and trim any extra wire.

11 Repeat steps 5 through 9 for the other earring.

12 Attach the ear wires to the empty loops at the ends of the shanks.

FIGURE 1

MATERIALS

2 deep-red faceted flat pears,* ½ inch (1.3 cm) diameter

2 deep-red faceted rondelles, 9 mm diameter

4 deep-red flat pears,* ⅜ inch (cm) diameter

8 deep-red round beads, 5 mm diameter

2 deep-red faceted rondelles, 10 mm diameter

26-gauge sterling dead-soft silver wire, 6 feet (1.8 m) long

24-gauge sterling dead-soft silver wire, 8 inches (20.3 cm) long

2 sterling silver lever-back ear wires

Flat pears are sometimes called briolettes.

Ruby Wave Bracelet

Chris Orcutt, Designer

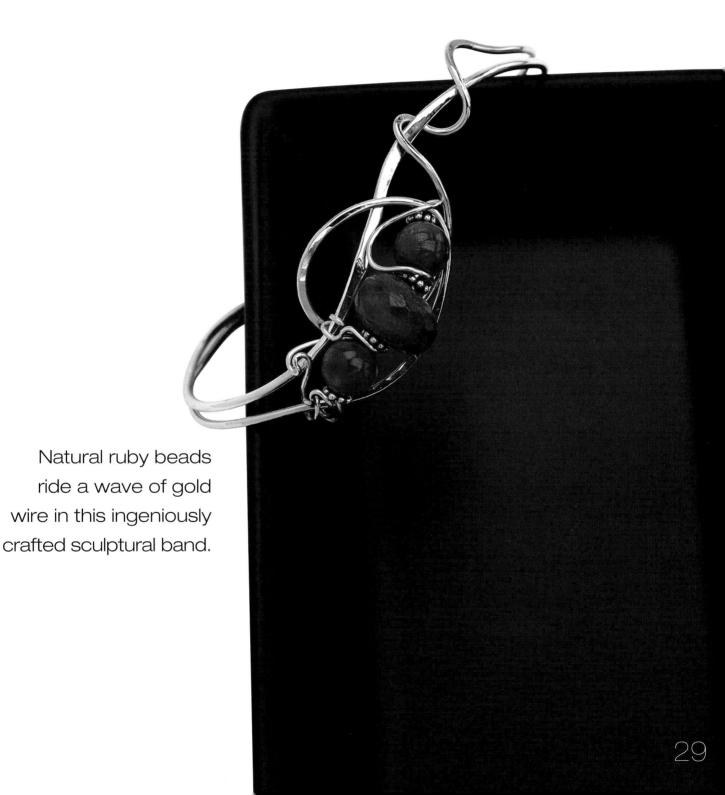

Natural ruby beads ride a wave of gold wire in this ingeniously crafted sculptural band.

Ruby Wave
Bracelet

MATERIALS

2 round natural ruby beads,
   8 mm diameter

1 natural ruby faceted rondelle,
   12 mm diameter

4 oxidized Bali sterling silver spacer
   beads, 2 x 6.9 mm

14-gauge dead-soft sterling silver wire,
   12 inches (30.5 cm) long

16-gauge dead-soft gold-filled wire,
   12 inches (30.5 cm) long

20-gauge dead-soft gold-filled wire,
   6 inches (15.2 cm) long

TOOLS

Ball-peen hammer and anvil

Bracelet mandrel

Plastic mallet

INSTRUCTIONS

1 Shape the center area of the 14-gauge wire into a gentle curve with round-nose pliers.

2 Use a ball-peen hammer and a jeweler's anvil to flatten the curved area.

3 Keeping one end each of the sterling silver and the 16-gauge gold-filled wires together in your hand, shape the gold wire into curves and loops over and around the silver wire, and use your fingers and round-nose pliers to wrap a large loop close to the center of the bracelet.

4 Once you're satisfied with the design, flatten a portion of the large gold loop as you did for the silver wire in step 2.

5 With your fingers or flat-nose pliers, twist the silver wire at the ends of the bracelet several times around the gold-filled one. Squeeze the bracelet ends (including the twists) with flat-nose pliers. Round off the cut ends with a fine file.

6 String the beads onto the 20-gauge gold-filled wire, starting and ending with a sterling silver spacer and using a spacer between each bead. Slide the beads to the middle of the wire.

7 Secure the beaded wire to the bracelet form with a few pleasing-looking loops, making sure to pass it between the spacers and the beads. Snip off any excess wire and tuck in the ends among the beads.

8 Form the bracelet over a bracelet mandrel and tap it into shape with a plastic mallet. Give the piece a final polish with a soft cloth or jewelry-polishing material.

Beaded Channel Ring

Dianne Karg Baron, Designer

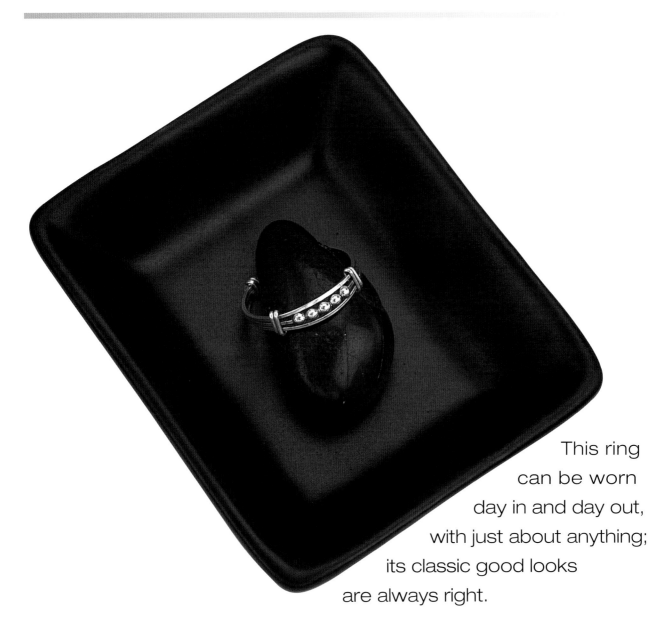

This ring
can be worn
day in and day out,
with just about anything;
its classic good looks
are always right.

Beaded Channel Ring

INSTRUCTIONS

Note: You'll need enough wire to wrap the mandrel three times at the next-larger ring size, plus a bit of extra. You can use some string or a paper strip to find the right length.

1 Clean and straighten the square wire by pulling it through the rouge cloth. Tightly coil the wire around the narrow end of the mandrel, keeping it perpendicular to the tool as you go. To enlarge the coil, push it gently down the mandrel, twisting the tool as you work; periodically remove the coil, flip it over, and replace it on the mandrel, then continue enlarging it. Increase the diameter of the coil until it's one size larger than the ring size you wish to make. There should be three revolutions of wire all around it.

2 Use a permanent marker to draw lines where the ends of the wire crisscross. This line represents the bottom of the ring. Mark another line on the opposite side of the coil to represent the top of the ring. Remove the ring from the mandrel.

3 Thread the beads onto one of the wire ends and move them around the coil until they're positioned at the wire's midpoint. Wrap a piece of masking tape around the beads and shank to hold the beads in place. Measure and mark two lines, each ³⁄₁₆ inch (0.5 cm) long, on either side of the bottom line.

4 Using flat-nose pliers, grasp the shank parallel to one of the new marks. Bend one of the ends of the wire 90 degrees across the exterior of the shank, doing so at the mark closest to it, then wrap the wire around the shank twice. Trim it on the interior of the shank and press it tightly against the band, using flat-nose pliers. Repeat at the other mark with the other end of the wire.

5 Slide the ring onto the mandrel and apply pressure to even up its shape. Remove the masking tape and set the ring aside.

6 Using the rouge cloth, clean and straighten the half-round wire. Placing it at one end of the line of beads, and with the flat part of the wire facing in, wrap the wire around the band twice. Trim any extra wire from the inside of the ring, file its tip with a needle file, and press it flat with flat-nose pliers.

7 Repeat step 6 on the other end of the line of beads before removing the masking tape.

MATERIALS

5 round silver beads, 2 mm diameter

22-gauge soft square wire, for the ring's band (see Note, above)

22-gauge half-hard half-round wire, 2 inches (5 cm) long, for the wraps

TOOLS

Rouge cloth

Wooden ring mandrel

Masking tape

Chui Necklace

Andrea L. McLester, Designer

A bright mix
of shapes
and textures
abounds in this
African-inspired creation, which is named after the
Swahili word for "leopard." The chain, made from handmade jump rings, has just the right visual weight to
complement its spiraled-wire pendants.

Chui Necklace

MATERIALS

6 brown glass seed beads

6 sterling silver saucer-shaped beads,
5 mm diameter

3 vintage red glass spacers, 4 mm thick

1 lampworked cylinder bead, ¾ inch
(1.9 cm) long

2 palm-wood bi-cone beads, each
½ x ⅞ inch (1.3 x 2.2 cm) long

2 lampworked cylinder beads, ⅝ inch
(1.6 cm) long

2 round mother-of-pearl beads, 8 mm
diameter

16-gauge dead-soft sterling silver wire,
15 feet (4.6 m) long

20-gauge dead-soft sterling silver wire,
5 feet (1.5 m) long

1 sterling silver toggle clasp

TOOLS

2 pairs of needle-nose pliers with non-
serrated or plastic-coated jaws

¼-inch (0.6 cm) dowel or similar object
to use as a mandrel

FINISHED LENGTH

20 inches (50.8 cm)

INSTRUCTIONS

Note: Adjust the length of the necklace if desired; it takes 6 jump rings, made from 16-gauge wire on a ¼-inch (0.6 cm) dowel, to make 1 inch (2.5 cm) of chain.

1 To make a handmade chain, make a coil roughly 3 inches (7.6 cm) long on the dowel with the 16-gauge wire. Remove the coil and use wire cutters to cut 116 rings from the coil's length.

2 Using the needle-nose pliers, close half the rings.

3 Thread one open ring through two closed ones.

4 Use an open ring to join a closed ring to one end of the short bit of chain you made in step 3. Close the open ring. Repeat this process until you've used all but two of your rings. Use the final two rings to attach your toggle clasp to the ends of the chain.

5 Use wire cutters to cut 10 pieces of 6-inch (15.2 cm), 20-gauge wire. Make 10 spiral head pins (the spiral technique is described on page 5); four full turns should be sufficient. These will be used to make beaded pendants.

6 Thread 1 seed bead, 1 silver saucer, 1 red spacer, another saucer, and another seed bead onto a spiral head pin. Using round-nose pliers, make a small loop at the top of this bead that is perpendicular to the spiral. Trim any excess wire. Thread the small loop onto the outermost wrap of another spiral head pin. You may need to loosen the last wrap a bit so the pendant can hang properly from it. Add the ¾-inch (1.9 cm) cylinder bead to this second spiral head pin. Make a loop at the top of this bead and trim any excess wire. Attach this jointed pendant to the center link in your chain, carefully opening the loop in the same way you would a jump ring.

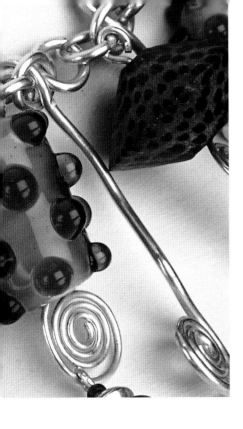

7 Cut a 6-inch (15.2 cm) piece of 16-gauge wire. Create a large spiral on one end, turning it three times. Thread the spiral through the second link from the center pendant and make another small spiral at the top, turning this spiral one and a half turns in the direction opposite that of the large spiral. To make it more visually interesting, use your thumb and forefinger to make the straight portion of the wire slightly wavy, until this short pendant is 1¾ inches (4.4 cm) long. Make another wavy-wire piece for the other side of the center pendant.

8 Make two more beaded pendants as described in step 6, using bi-cone beads instead of cylinders. Attach them to the chain, on either side of the wavy wire pendants, skipping a link between them.

9 Make and attach two more wavy-wire pendants, as you did in step 7. If necessary, make additional turns to the lower spiral so that it's approximately 1¼ inches (3.2 cm) long.

10 Thread one of the smaller cylinder beads onto a spiral head pin. Make a loop at the top of the bead. Repeat to make a second pendant. Attach the small loops to the chains as before.

11 Make another pair of wavy-wire spirals from 6-inch (15.2 cm) pieces of 16-gauge wire, turning them each four times. Attach them as before, closing with a small spiral at the top. These pendants should be approximately 1 inch (2.5 cm) long. If necessary, make additional turns to the lower spiral to achieve this length.

12 Thread one mother-of-pearl bead onto each of the last two spiral head pins. Make loops at the tops of the beads and attach these outermost pendants to the chain.

This knitted-wire band with brightly colored beads is a party on your wrist. Pair it with the same designer's Festive Spiral Earrings on page 58 for an especially lively set.

Mardi Gras Bracelet

Rachel Dow, Designer

MATERIALS

95 gemstone and freshwater pearl beads in complementary colors, 4 to 6 mm diameter

26-gauge dead-soft gold-filled wire, 15 feet (4.6 m) long

10 sterling silver jump rings, 4 mm diameter

1 sterling silver 5-ring multistrand slide clasp

TOOLS

Knitting needles, 2.25 mm (size 1 U.S.)

FINISHED LENGTH

7 inches (17.8 cm)

INSTRUCTIONS

Note: Standard knitting abbreviations are used. After you have finished each row, pull the knitted strip down and reshape it. Make sure not to kink the wire. Use chain-nose pliers to straighten it out if you do.

1 Thread all the beads onto the wire.

Loosely CO 5 sts.

Row 1: K without adding any beads.

Row 2: P, adding beads randomly.

Alternate rows of k and p, adding beads randomly, until the band measures 7 inches (17.8 cm) long. The last row should be k without any beads added.

BO sts. Weave in both tail ends of the wire.

2 Place five evenly spaced jump rings along a short end of the band, slipping each ring through two strands of wire. Attach each jump ring to a ring on one of the clasp elements. Attach the other short end of the band to the other clasp element in the same way.

Make these gleaming post-style pierced earrings in a flash. Two versions are shown here: one with pearls and another pair made with paua shell beads, both ingenious interpretations of an all-one-piece design.

Pearly Spirally Post Earrings

Hanni Yothers, Designer

MATERIALS

2 gray button pearls, 4 x 7 mm (or use paua shell beads)

22-gauge, half-hard 14-karat gold-filled wire, 8 inches (20.3 cm) long

2 14-karat gold-filled ear nuts

INSTRUCTIONS

1 Cut the wire into two 1½-inch (3.8 cm) pieces and two 2½ inch (6.4 cm) pieces.

2 Make a spiral from a 1½-inch (3.8 cm) piece of wire, until it's at least ³⁄₁₆ inch (0.5 cm) but not more than ¼ inch (0.6 cm) wide. Trim any remaining wire and file any sharp edges. Repeat the process with the second piece of 1½ inch (3.8 cm) wire.

3 Using your chain-nose pliers, make a 90-degree bend ¾ inch (1.9 cm) from the end of a 2½-inch (6.4 cm) piece of wire. This will be the earring's post. Thread one of the spirals you made in step 2 onto the short section of the wire, until it touches the bend, followed by a pearl (with the round side facing the spiral).

4 Use your thumb and middle finger (it's sometimes hard to hang on to) to grasp the pearl. Keep the long wire pointing up, pushing on it with your index finger near the bend in order to keep the pearl and spiral flush against the wire bend. With your other hand, grasp the long wire and pull it as tightly as possible over the top and down the back of the pearl. Wrap the long wire around the post wire, as close to the back of the pearl as possible. Keep each wrap tight against the previous one. Cut the wire when this spiral looks the same as the one on the front of the earring.

5 File any sharp edges on the spiral wrap and on the post that extends straight out from the pearl. File a tiny notch all the way around the post to keep the ear nut securely on it.

6 Repeat steps 3 through 5 for the second earring.

Dynamic silver coils
hold a row of tiny
faceted beads in this
wonderfully simple
bangle that recalls the
ankle bracelets of India.

Marie Lee Carter, Designer

Rajah Bangle

MATERIALS

10 faceted round beads, 4 mm diameter*

14-gauge sterling silver wire, 8 inches (20.3 cm) long, for the bracelet's armature

22-gauge sterling silver wire, 80 inches (2 m) long, for the wrap

20-gauge sterling silver wire, 75 inches (1.9 m) long, for the wrap

The holes must be large enough to accommodate 22-gauge wire.

TOOLS

Pliers with plastic-coated jaws

Ball-peen hammer and block

Bent chain-nose pliers

Plastic mallet

Bracelet mandrel (a baseball bat is a fine substitute)

INSTRUCTIONS

Note: Makes one bracelet

1 Straighten the 14-gauge wire by gently pulling it through plastic-coated pliers. Use a ball-peen hammer to flatten each end of the wire (three or four taps should do it). Make a loop at each end with round-nose pliers. Bend them back a bit, to center them over the straight part of the wire. Mark the center of the wire with a permanent marker, then make a mark 1 inch (2.5 cm) from each side of the center point.

2 Put on eye protection to shield yourself as you work with the long pieces of wire. Starting at one loop, wrap the 22-gauge wire onto the 14-gauge wire. When you reach the first mark, thread a bead onto the 22-gauge wire, then hold it there as you make three more wraps. Add another bead and wrap as before, until you've used all the beads; finish wrapping the rest of the 14-gauge wire. Snip the end of the 22-gauge wire and press it into the coils with the bent chain-nose pliers. File any rough edges.

3 Wrap the 20-gauge wire over the 22-gauge wire. At the section with the beads, make two wraps between each bead, checking your work for uniformity. Finish as you did in step 2.

4 Create the hook of the clasp by prying open a loop on one end of the bangle with round-nose pliers. Grasp the hook with flat-nose pliers and turn it 90 degrees. Carefully file any rough edges. Slightly taper the tip of the hook.

5 With the plastic mallet, tap the bangle gently (avoiding the beads, which should face out) against the mandrel until it has a satisfactory shape.

6 Make sure that the hook fits into the loop that serves as the eye, gently twisting either as necessary.

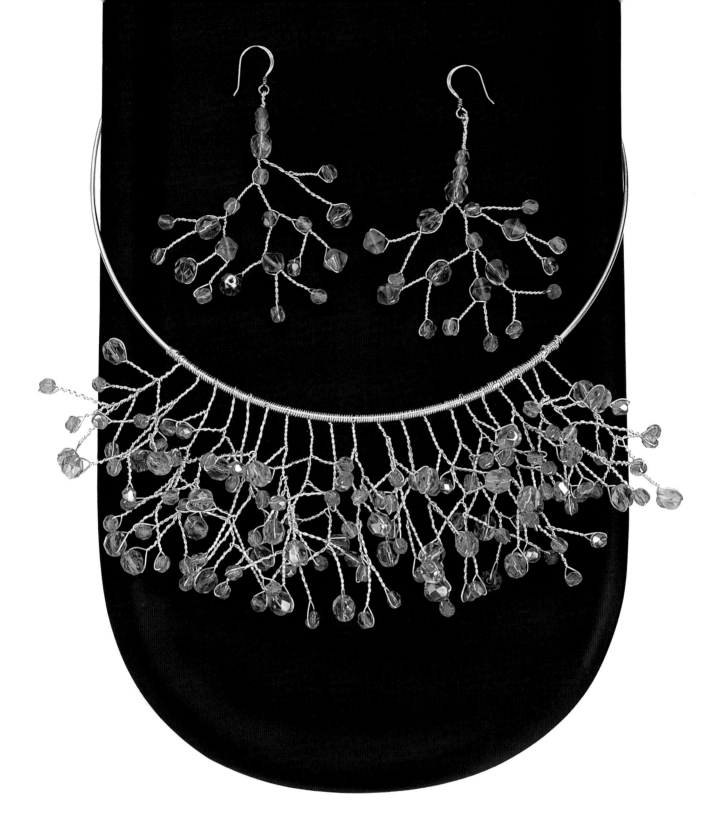

These delicate accessories
feature tiny turquoise facets that
shimmer on twisted silver wire.

Turquoise Twists Necklace and Earrings

Marinda Stewart, Designer

MATERIALS FOR THE NECKLACE

120 turquoise faceted glass beads, 4 mm and 6 mm diameter

26-gauge silver-tone wire, 10 yards (9.1 m) long

1 silver neck ring

INSTRUCTIONS

1 Thread all the beads onto the wire in random order. Wrap one end of the wire tightly onto the neck ring for ½ inch (1.3 cm).

2 With a permanent marker, make a mark 20 inches (50.8 cm) from where the wire comes off the neck ring. Fold this section of wire in half and slide the first bead into the fold. "Capture" it by twisting the wires together for approximately ½ inch (1.3 cm). Slide the next bead 1½ inches (3.8 cm) away from the base of the first twist and capture the bead by twisting the wire halves together for about ¾ inch (1.9 cm). Bring the next loose bead to the base of the last twist, create another twist, and create a "branch" there, as shown in figure 1. Working in turn with each loose bead on the untwisted wire, randomly twist beaded branches with two or three arms on each until you've used six or seven beads.

3 Wrap the neck ring tightly without beads for ¼ to ⅜ inch (0.6 to 1 cm). You should have used most of the 20 inches of wire that you had marked in step 2.

FIGURE **1**

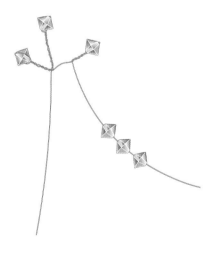

Turquoise Twists Necklace and Earrings

4 Repeat steps 2 and 3 to make a total of 18 branches. End with a ½-inch (1.3 cm) wrap as at the beginning of the ring. Trim any excess wire.

5 Arrange the arms so all the beads point down. If necessary, carefully slide the branches along the neck wire to center them.

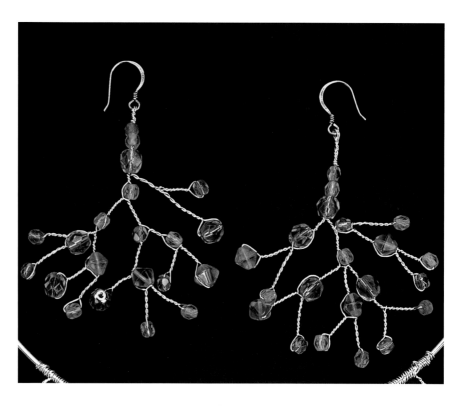

MATERIALS FOR THE EARRINGS

42 turquoise faceted glass beads, 4 and 6 mm diameter

26-gauge silver-colored wire, 48 inches (1.2 m) long

2 ear wires

INSTRUCTIONS

MAKE 2.

1 Cut a piece of wire 24 inches (61 cm) long. String 19 beads of both sizes randomly on it and knot the ends so the beads stay on. As with the necklace, twist the wire, with beads captured in it, into a pair of opposed branches.

2 Cut off the knots at the ends of the wires. Fold the branches together in the middle and twist. Thread a 6-mm and a pair of 4-mm beads onto this twisted wire. Attach an ear wire to the earring using a wrapped-loop finish. Trim any excess wire.

Santa Fe Cuff

Michaelanne Hall, Designer

This cuff proves that less really is more. Its design incorporates both linear and circular forms, and the use of turquoise lends its style a southwestern touch.

Santa Fe Cuff

MATERIALS

5 gold-filled round beads,
   4 mm diameter

24 turquoise round beads,
   4 mm diameter

20-gauge half-hard sterling silver
   square wire, 31 inches (78.7 cm)
   long, for the cuff's exterior and
   the hook

20-gauge half-hard 14-karat gold-filled
   square wire, 26 inches (66 cm) long,
   for the cuff's interior

24-gauge half-hard 14-karat gold-filled
   square wire, 6½ inches (16.5 cm)
   long, for stringing the beads

20-gauge half-hard 14-karat gold-filled
   half-round wire, 46 inches (1.2 m)
   long, for the wraps

TOOLS

Masking tape

INSTRUCTIONS

1 Straighten the silver wire, then cut one piece 15½ inches (39.4 cm) long and two pieces each 6½ inches (16.5 cm) long. Mark the center of the long piece with a permanent marker, center it in the jaws of flat-nose pliers, and bend both sides of the wire to make a U. Set aside these wires.

2 Cut the 20-gauge gold-filled square wire into four pieces, each 6½ inches (16.5 cm) long. Mark ½ inch (1.3 cm) from each end. Use a pin vise to twist all four pieces of wire between the marks, leaving the ends untwisted.

3 String all the beads on the 24-gauge wire, alternating four turquoise beads with a gold one.

4 Place the U-shaped silver wire from step 1 on your work surface; its legs will be the outermost wire of the cuff. Place all the 6½-inch (16.5 cm) wires between the legs and parallel to each other, alternating the twisted wires with the silver ones; put the beaded wire in the middle. Align the ends of the seven straight wires ¼ inch (0.6 cm) away from the U-shaped bend. Use masking tape to secure all the wires on each end, keeping the square wires flat.

5 Mark the interior wires at their midpoints. Center the third gold bead from the end on this midpoint mark.

6 Cut 10 pieces of 20-gauge half-round wire, each 3 inches (7.6 cm) long. Use needle-nose pliers to make a hook at one end of each piece.

7 Working directly next to the center gold bead, hook the sharp bend of one of the half-round wires over the silver outermost wire and, using needle-nose pliers, make three wraps around the bundle of wires. Trim it and finish by hooking the end to the inside.

8 Slide four turquoise beads against the wire wrap you just made and, using the same method as before, wrap a piece of half-round wire on the other side of the beads to frame them. Slide one gold bead against this wrap, then wrap another piece of half-round wire on the bead's other side. Repeat, leaving the last four turquoise beads on this side free. Repeat with the beads on the other side of the center gold bead.

9 Cut two pieces of half-round wire, each 18 inches (45.7 cm) long. Hook one piece next to the last set of four turquoise beads closest to the U-shaped bend in the silver wire. Wrap the half-round wire 16 to 18 times, until the ends of the interior parallel wires are no longer visible. Repeat on the other side, leaving the two outermost silver wires exposed.

10 Use flat-nose pliers to bend the outermost silver wires outward 45 degrees. Trim each to ⅜ inch (1 cm) long. Use round-nose pliers to roll them inward to make loops.

11 To make the hook for the clasp, cut a piece of square silver wire 2½ inches (6.4 cm) long. Bend it into a U shape. Using round-nose pliers held perpendicular to the wire, grasp the tip of the bend and angle it slightly. To form the hook, move your pliers to just beyond the angled tip and use your fingers to bend the wire ends around the outer part of the tool's tip. Now bend the ends of the wire outward 30 degrees. Mark ⅜ inch (1 cm) from each end and make a loop from that length of wire. Attach the hooks to the loops on the cuff.

12 Starting at the middle of the bracelet, slowly and gently shape its form until you can close the clasp.

Love Knot Earrings

Andrea L. McLester, Designer

Shifting angles of view make dichroic glass beads come alive in these show-stopping earrings. The coiled area may look challenging to make, but it's actually as easy as slipping keys on a key ring.

Love Knot Earrings

MATERIALS

10 disk-shaped dichroic glass spacer beads, ⅛ x ⅝ inches (0.3 x 1.6 cm)

8 saucer-shaped sterling silver beads, 5 mm diameter

20-gauge dead-soft sterling silver wire, 7 feet (2.1 m) long

2 French ear wires

TOOLS

⅜-inch (0.95 cm) dowel or other mandrel

INSTRUCTIONS

Note: The earrings' finished dimensions are 1½ x 3 inches (3.8 x 7.6 cm); for smaller-scale earrings, use smaller dowels and add more turns to the spirals on the crosspiece. Other components should be adjusted accordingly, so you may wish to make a sample earring using an inexpensive wire first.

1 Create the Love Knot by wrapping a 14-inch (35.6 cm) piece of 20-gauge wire around the dowel 12 times. Remove the coil from the dowel and trim any excess wire from the ends.

2 Gently grasping the ends of the coil, spread it so that the sixth wrap is exposed just enough to cut the coil neatly in half with flush cutters. Be careful not to spread the entire coil apart.

3 Carefully thread one coil through the other, as if adding a key to a split-ring key chain. Once the coils are entwined, spread their outer sides.

4 Cut a piece of wire 3 inches (7.6 cm) long. Using round-nose pliers, make a small wrapped loop at one end. Thread a dichroic bead on the wire; slip it through the center of the Love Knot, making sure that it passes straight through all its rings; and add another dichroic bead onto it. Use the round-nose pliers to make a long, oval-shaped wrapped loop, ½ inch (1.3 cm) from the last bead. This loop should be long enough to hold two pieces of 20-gauge wire lying side by side.

5 Repeat steps 1 through 4 to make a second knot assembly.

6 Connect the knot assemblies to ear wires by their loops.

7 Bend a 3-inch (7.6 cm) piece of wire at its center, so that it's shaped like a U. Thread this wire through the oval loop on one of the knot components. Insert both ends of the wire through a dichroic bead. Trim each end of the wire so that it extends no more than ⅜ inch (0.95 cm) from the bottom of the bead. Shape the ends of the wire into a pair of small, side-by-side loops that are perpendicular to the large loop above the bead. Repeat for the other earring.

8 For the center dangle, make a spiral with a 4-inch (10.2 cm) piece of wire, stopping when there's just ½ inch (1.3 cm) of wire left. Grasp the end of it and make a small loop in the direction opposite the spiral at the other end. Open the loop and thread it through the pair of side-by-side loops you created in step 7. Close the loop. Repeat for the other earring.

9 For the crosspiece, you'll need a 6½-inch (16.5 cm) piece of wire. Use a permanent marker to mark the center of the wire. Make a spiral until you are ¼ inch (0.6 cm) from the center mark.

10 Thread the crosspiece through the lower loop of the knot assembly. Make another spiral at the other end. If necessary, use needle-nose pliers to pinch the lower loop on the knot assembly so that the crosspiece rests above, not beside, the wire holding the center pendant.

11 Repeat steps 9 and 10 for the other earring.

12 For the side dangles, cut a 2-inch (5.1 cm) piece of wire and make a small loop at one end of it. (If you wish, you may substitute manufactured head pins.) Use needle-nose pliers to bend this loop 90 degrees. Thread a silver saucer bead, a dichroic bead, and another silver saucer bead onto the pin. Make a U-shaped bend ⅜ inch (1.0 cm) away from the last bead. Thread the wire through one of the crosspiece spirals and then close it with a wrapped loop, making sure the pendant swings freely. Repeat this step for the other dangle.

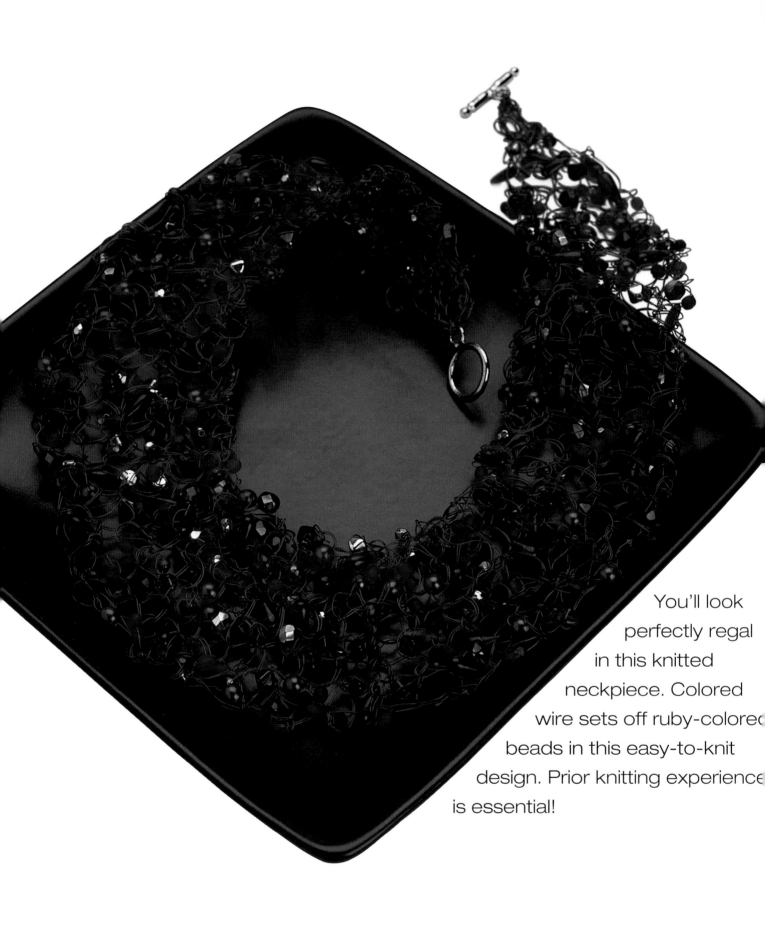

You'll look perfectly regal in this knitted neckpiece. Colored wire sets off ruby-colored beads in this easy-to-knit design. Prior knitting experience is essential!

Marinda Stewart, Designer

Cleopatra's Collar

MATERIALS

Red teardrops,* 3 and 6 mm diameter

Red pearls,* 6 mm diameter

Matte red faceted beads,*
    4 mm diameter

Transparent red faceted beads,*
    4 mm diameter

Transparent red faceted beads,*
    6 mm diameter

Red pyramid beads,* 6 mm diameter

2 spools of 28-gauge red craft wire,
    each with a minimum of 20 yards
    (18.3 m) of wire

1 toggle clasp

*You will need enough beads to string
    80 inches (2 m) of wire.*

TOOLS

Knitting needles, 10 mm (size 15 U.S.)

FINISHED LENGTH

25 inches (63.5 cm)

INSTRUCTIONS

Note: The designer recommends knitting in the Continental, rather than American, style.

1 String 40 inches (1 m) of beads in random order onto each spool of wire. Leave the bead-strung wire extended 20 yards (18.3 m) but still attached to the spools.

Working with the 2 wires tog, CO 3 sts, leaving a 4-inch (10.2 cm) tail.

Rows 1 & 2: K.

Row 3: Inc1, k3, inc1, for a total of 5 sts.

Row 4: K. As you work the first st, slide a bead from the first spool into the first st. For the next st, pull a bead from the second spool. Continue to alternate a bead from each spool with every st.

K every row until the work measures 19 inches (48.3 cm) long.

K 1 row without any beads.

For the next row, dec1, k3, dec1, to make 3 sts.

K for 2 rows.

BO. Cut all of the extra wire, leaving 4-inch (10.2 cm) tails.

2 Secure each wire end to one half of the toggle by wrapping it repeatedly through the first row of stitches and through the toggle's loop. Weave any excess wire through the work; bury the ends in the stitches.

3 Contour the necklace to your neck by compressing the stitches on the inside edge and stretching those on the outer edge.

Carnelian beads and gold wire combine to create gorgeous earrings reminiscent of the wares of Far Eastern markets. The designer's fine wirework has the appearance of filigree.

Bollywood Dreams Earrings

Eni Oken, Designer

MATERIALS

12 round beads, 7 mm diameter

2 top-drilled faceted flat pear carnelian beads,* ½ inch (1.3 cm) long

20 round carnelian seed beads, 3 mm diameter

2 round carnelian beads, 5 mm diameter

26-gauge gold-filled dead-soft wire, 9 feet (2.7 m) long, for the wraps

18-gauge gold-filled dead-soft wire, 7½ inches (19 cm) long, for the teardrop-shaped element

2 gold-filled lever-back ear wires

* Faceted flat pear beads are sometimes called briolettes.

TOOLS

Wooden dowel or pen, ¾ inch (1.9 cm) diameter

Mallet or hammer

Anvil

INSTRUCTIONS

MAKE 2.

1 Cut 6 pieces of 26-gauge wire, each 3 inches (7.6 cm) long. Make eye pins with tiny wrapped loops out of each of them, then slip a 7-mm round bead onto each. Close the open ends with another miniscule wrapped loop. Cut off any excess wire.

2 Cut the 18-gauge wire in half. Working with one piece, form small loops at both ends of it. Using the wooden dowel and your fingers, form the wire into a teardrop shape. Flatten the shape on an anvil with a mallet or hammer until it's work hardened.

3 To create the flat-pear dangles at the earring's center, cut a piece of 26-gauge wire, 3 inches (7.6 cm) long. Place a flat pear on it, leaving a tail 1 inch (2.5 cm) long on one side; wrap the shorter wire around the longer one several times. Trim the short end of the wire. Now use round-nose pliers to form a small wrapped loop from the remaining wire, making the loop as close as possible to the wrapping you just did and winding some of the excess wire on top of the existing wrapping. Trim the wire closely.

4 To assemble all the elements, cut a piece of 26-gauge wire 2½ feet (76.2 cm) long. Leaving a 1-inch-long (2.5 cm) tail to help you hold onto it, start at one of the loops on the teardrop shape and tightly coil the wire to one of the loops for ¼ inch (0.6 cm); trim the tail. Slip a seed bead onto the working wire, making sure the bead is positioned at the outermost edge of the wire teardrop, and continue coiling another 3/16 inch (0.5 cm). Add another seed bead to the working wire and coil another 3/16 inch (0.5 cm). Now slip a seed bead and one of the dangles you made in step 1 onto the working wire. Continue to wrap the wire and add the seed beads and dangles in this way until you've attached them all. After you finish, if the beads aren't symmetrically spaced on the teardrop, spread out the coils a bit until they are.

5 Bring together the two loops of the teardrop element so that one is atop the other, then wrap them together twice tightly. Form a small cap by wrapping the shoulders of the teardrop, below the loops, six more times. On the last wrap, slip the flat pear dangle onto the working wire, then use round-nose pliers to twist a small wrapped loop that faces into the center of the teardrop shape. Finish by tightly coiling it around the teardrop wire, near the cap. Trim any excess wire.

6 Using a 3-inch (7.6 cm) length of 26-gauge wire and a 5-mm bead, make a wrapped bead loop link that connects one of its loop to the two joined loops above the cap, and the other one in an ear wire.

Beware of gazing at this bold ring for too long—the designer's sleek brass wirework is just as mesmerizing as its central pearl.

Hypnosis Ring

Joanna Gollberg, Designer

MATERIALS

1 half-drilled bead or pearl,
   4 mm diameter

12-gauge brass wire, 6 inches
   (15.2 cm) long

Extra-strength glue

TOOLS

Ring mandrel

INSTRUCTIONS

1 Make a 90-degree bend in the wire, ¼ inch (0.6 cm) away from its end. While holding the tail end of the bend in flat-nose pliers, completely wrap the wire once around the mandrel at your ring size.

2 File the tip of the bend to make the wire thinner, until it fits into the hole of the bead or pearl like a peg. Make sure to leave the wire thick near the crook of the bend, because you'll need to grasp it there when you make the spiral.

3 To make the spiral, carefully hold the peg with flat-nose pliers so you don't break it off. Use your fingers to fashion the long end of the wire into a spiral that's perpendicular to the peg. Continue until the spiral is the size you desire, then cut off any excess wire and file the end.

4 Put a small dot of extra-strength glue on the peg, then gently place the half-drilled bead or pearl on it. Allow the glue to dry.

The carved amethyst beads and golden fringes of these super-simple earrings evoke swaying paper lanterns of the Orient.

Kate Drew-Wilkinson, Designer

Lantern Earrings

MATERIALS

4 round beads, 14-karat gold filled, 2.5 mm diameter

8 spacers, 14-karat gold filled, 2.5 mm diameter

4 turquoise beads, 6 mm diameter

4 spacers, 14-karat gold filled, 4 mm diameter

2 carved amethyst oval beads, 10 x 15 mm

4 round beads, 14-karat gold filled, 2 mm diameter

2 turquoise beads, 4 mm diameter

22-gauge half-hard 14-karat gold-filled wire, 9 inches (22.9 cm) long

14-karat gold-filled 1 mm flat chain, 16 inches (40.6 cm) long

2 gold jump rings, 5 mm diameter

2 14-karat gold-filled ear wires

INSTRUCTIONS

MAKE 2.

1 Cut six segments of chain that range in length from ¾ to 1¾ inches (1.9 to 4.4 cm).

2 Cut a piece of wire 3 inches (7.6 cm) long. Fashion it into a wrapped bead loop link, catching one end of all the pieces of chain in one loop and stringing beads onto it in the following sequence: 2.5-mm round, 2.5-mm spacer, 6-mm turquoise, 4-mm spacer, amethyst, 4-mm spacer, 6-mm turquoise, 2.5-mm spacer, and 2.5-mm round. Cut off any extra wire.

3 Cut a piece of wire 1½ inches (3.8 cm) long. Make a wrapped bead loop link with beads in the following sequence: 2-mm round, 2.5-mm spacer, 4-mm turquoise, 2.5-mm spacer, and 2-mm round. Trim off the extra wire.

4 Attach the two bead links to each other with a jump ring. Connect the ear wire to the shorter bead link.

The dynamic spiral shape and brightly colored beads of these earrings are sure to attract attention at parties, or simply enhance an upbeat mood.

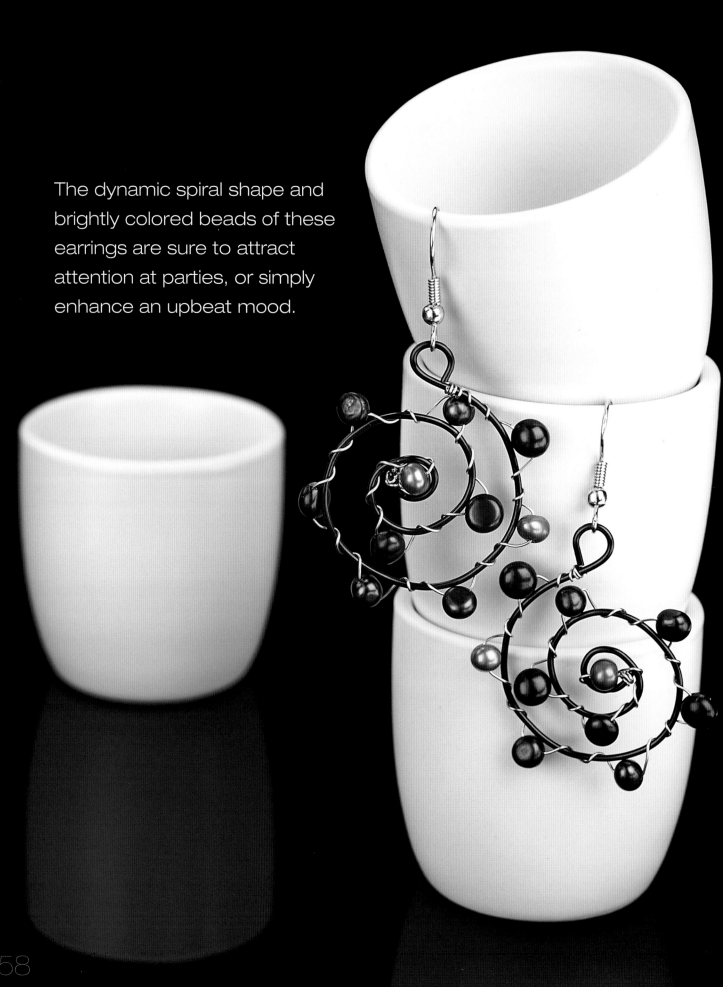

Festive Spiral Earrings

Rachel Dow, Designer

MATERIALS

10 pairs of round or button-shaped freshwater pearl beads in various colors, 4 mm diameter

2 pieces of 18-gauge colored wire, each 6½ inches (16.5 cm) long, for the armature

2 pieces of 26-gauge dead-soft gold-filled wire, each 10¼ inches (26 cm) long, for the wrap

2 gold-tone ear wires

INSTRUCTIONS

MAKE 2

Note: Match the sizes, shapes, and color patterns of the beads.

1 Straighten out the 18-gauge wire. Make a closed loop at the end of the wire. Grasp the loop with the widest part of a pair of chain-nose pliers and, holding your pliers hand stationary, rotate the wire into a loose spiral shape, leaving ½ inch (1.3 cm) of the tail end of the wire remaining.

2 Make another loop in the opposite direction as the spiral, with the remaining tail end of the wire. As you work, align it with the loop at the spiral's center. Trim any extra length of the wire that's left.

3 Secure the 26-gauge wire around the center loop in the spiral, slip on a bead, and tuck it into the spiral's loop. Hold the bead in place and wrap the wire twice around the spiral.

4 Add nine more beads, leaving a little bit of spacing between each one. As you work, make sure that your wrapping is tight and that the beads are snug against the spiral without distorting its shape. Straighten any kinks with chain-nose pliers. Finish by wrapping the lighter wire three times tightly around the base of the spiral's outer loop. Snip off any extra wire. When you wrap the second spiral, make a mirror-image earring by working on the opposite side and in the opposite direction as the first one.

5 Attach the gold-tone ear wires to the earrings' exterior loops.

Here's a lighthearted, uncomplicated bracelet that's so easy to fashion you can make several in various colors for party favors—or wear them all yourself, gypsy style.

Jellyroll Bracelet

Andrea L. McLester, Designer

MATERIALS

3 disk-shaped resin beads, ⅝ inch
(1.6 cm) diameter

3 pieces of 20-gauge anodized wire,
each 14 inches (35.6 cm) long, for
the jellyroll links

3 pieces of 20-gauge anodized wire,
each 2½ inches (6.4 cm) long, for
the wrapped bead loop links

2 pieces of 20-gauge anodized wire,
each 7 inches (17.8 cm) long, for
the clasp

TOOLS

½-inch (1.3 cm) dowel or other
mandrel

Round-nose pliers with plastic-coated
jaws

FINISHED LENGTH

8¾ inches (22.2 cm)

INSTRUCTIONS

Note: Be aware that the colored coating
on anodized and plated wires is soft and
can be easily scratched. If you don't have
the plastic-coated pliers, wrap your
regular ones with plastic tape.

1 To make a jellyroll link, use round-
nose pliers to make a 90-degree bend
in a 14-inch (35.6 cm) length of wire,
2 inches (5 cm) from one end. Grasp the
long end of the wire at the bend so that
the pliers' jaws lie parallel to the bent part
of the wire (see figure 1). Keeping the wire
near the tip of the pliers' jaws, make a
spiral until you have 7 inches (17.8 cm) of
wire left. The short piece of wire will be
standing straight out from the center of
the spiral.

2 Using the round-nose pliers, bend
the longer section of wire 90
degrees, 2 inches (5.1 cm) from the end,
but in the direction opposite that of the
bend you made in step 1.

3 Make another spiral at this end of
the wire, rolling it in the opposite
direction as the first, until the second
roll is ½ inch (1.3 cm) from the first.

4 Bend both short ends of the wire, in
the same direction, so they lie flat
over the spirals. Fold the spirals together,
with these short wires to the inside. Coil

FIGURE **1**

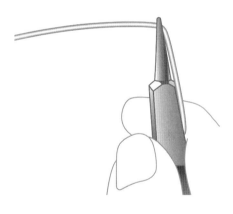

61

Jellyroll Bracelet

them until they are aligned, one over the other, forming a double-sided "jellyroll" link. See figure 2 for an exploded view of what the element should look like. Make wrapped loops on both ends of the wire.

5 Repeat steps 1 through 4 to make three more jellyroll links.

6 Make a wrapped bead loop link with a resin bead on a 2½-inch (6.4 cm) piece of wire. Before closing each loop, thread a jellyroll link on it. Cut off any excess wire. Repeat at the other end.

7 Connect the two sections with a wrapped bead loop link.

8 To make the eye of the clasp, use a 7-inch (17.8 cm) piece of wire. Make a wrapped loop over the dowel, wrapping the wire twice around it. Thread a resin bead onto the wire, then make a wrapped loop on the other end, slipping a jellyroll link onto the loop before closing it.

9 To make the hook, fold the last piece of wire double, with one end 2 inches (5.1 cm) longer than the other. Do not trim the ends. Use your thumb to fold the bent end of the wire over the dowel. Grasp the folded end of the wire with round-nose pliers and make a loose spiral.

10 Slip the free end of the wire into the loop of the last jellyroll link, then make an extra-long wrapped loop out of the rest of the wire.

FIGURE 2

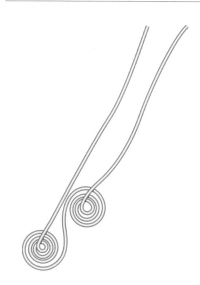

Key to Wire Gauges

The projects in this book were made using wire manufactured in the United States, whose standards for wire diameters differ from those in the British system. AWG is the acronym for American, or Brown & Sharpe, wire gauge sizes and their equivalent rounded metric measurements. SWG is the acronym for the British Standard, or Imperial, system in the UK. Refer to the chart below if you use SWG wire. Only part of the full range of wire gauges that are available from jewelry suppliers is included here.

AWG IN.	AWG MM	GAUGE	SWG IN.	SWG MM
0.204	5.18	4	0.232	5.89
0.182	4.62	5	0.212	5.38
0.162	4.12	6	0.192	4.88
0.144	3.66	7	0.176	4.47
0.129	3.28	8	0.160	4.06
0.114	2.90	9	0.144	3.66
0.102	2.59	10	0.128	3.25
0.091	2.31	11	0.116	2.95
0.081	2.06	12	0.104	2.64
0.072	1.83	13	0.092	2.34
0.064	1.63	14	0.080	2.03
0.057	1.45	15	0.072	1.83
0.051	1.30	16	0.064	1.63
0.045	1.14	17	0.056	1.42
0.040	1.02	18	0.048	1.22
0.036	0.914	19	0.040	1.02
0.032	0.813	20	0.036	0.914
0.029	0.737	21	0.032	0.813
0.025	0.635	22	0.028	0.711
0.023	0.584	23	0.024	0.610
0.020	0.508	24	0.022	0.559
0.018	0.457	25	0.020	0.508
0.016	0.406	26	0.018	0.457

Ruby Wave Bracelet, page 29

About the Designers

Dianne Karg Baron has exhibited and published internationally. She's a past president of the Metal Arts Guild of Canada and International Guild of Wire Jewelry Artists. Visit the website online at www.wrapturewirejewellery.on.ca for more.

Marie Lee Carter's career began in a metalsmithing class at the Fashion Institute of Technology in NY. She tells stories in precious metal and stone. See her work at www.mariecarter.etsy.com and www.mariecarter.1000markets.com.

Rachel Dow fabricates sterling silver, metal clay, and found object jewelry. She also makes handspun, hand-dyed yarn. Her work is in selected galleries and at www.rmddesigns.com.

Kate Drew-Wilkinson was an actress, but became fascinated by the history and magic of beads. She's written books and articles on bead jewelry, makes instructional films, and teaches bead making and jewelry design in Europe.

Ellen Gerritse traveled extensively, teaching fine arts in Europe and Asia. She creates objects from accessible materials and tools.

She won the Collectors' Choice Award during the Mind over Metal show in Houston, TX.

Joanna Gollberg is a studio jeweler who's authored four books including *The Ultimate Jeweler's Guide*. She teaches jewelry making at craft schools and for metalsmithing groups. See her work online at www.joannagollberg.com.

Michaelanne Hall is a self-taught artist living in Asheville, NC. She sells her jewelry in a local gallery.

Mami Laher loves originality and uniqueness in creativity. She makes bead and wire jewelry with basic tools. Originally from Japan, she now resides in Los Angeles. See more at www.mamibeads.com.

Andrea L. McLester created jewelry for legendary ballerinas and opera singers as a theatrical designer and costumer. She now lives in Temple, TX. See her work and a list of galleries at www.andreamclester.com.

Eni Oken's jewelry embraces fantasy art, sculpture, architecture, and lace-making techniques in intricate designs. Originally from Brazil, she now explores techniques in L.A. Visit www.jewelrylessons.com.

Chris Orcutt fabricates one-of-a-kind jewelry by hand. She's a goldsmith/jewelry designer at the Metal Waterfall Gallery and Christine Ann Jewelry in Leavenworth, WA. Visit www.rubylane.com/shops/christineannjewelry.

Carolyn Skei works in polymer jewelry, fiber arts, papermaking, bookbinding, and experimental photography. She's taught for Dallas area institutions. Her work has won recognition in the Dallas Quilt Celebration and the Visual Arts Society of Texas.

Marinda Stewart is a designer and teacher who authored *Punchneedle: The Complete Guide*. She's appeared on TV and contributed to magazines and books. Her work is in museums and galleries. See www.marindastewart.com.

Hanni Yothers grew up surrounded by nature. When she learned that stones and metal create beautiful jewelry, she began designing, creating, and selling jewelry. View her jewelry at www.heyjewelry.com.

Others in the Simply Series